About the Author

Debbie Hardy holds a BA degree in Fine Arts, and Certifications in Crystal Healing, Advanced Crystal Master, Reiki Master, and Angel Therapy. She is also a lifetime member of the World Metaphysical Association. She has found a deep love and connection to working with crystals. She is also an advocate for meditation and wishes to spread the word to everyone around the world that meditation can be easy and the benefits are unlimited. She started her own crystal therapy business which included a crystal boutique. Eventually she was drawn to transition to focus completely on distance healing sessions and online sales. However she continues to hold in person workshops and online meditations to teach others the benefits of crystals and meditation. She lives in Southern California with her husband, daughter and two dogs, Penny and JJ, who are a big part of the family.

www.hardycrystalblessing.com

ISBN 9781979776479

Debbie Hardy © 2017
Debbie Hardy © 2019 Revised
Cover image by Elisa Lee

Disclaimer

The author is not a medical practitioner, cannot give medical or psychological advice or diagnose patients, and cannot prescribe medications. Please consult your licensed medical practitioner if you have any health or psychological concerns. The information provided in this book does not constitute and is not a substitute for medical advice. Please be advised there are no guarantees that the following content will "heal" your specific situation and there are no guarantees of specific results from following the guidance of the content provided in this book. Information provided in this book is as accurate as possible; however, the author accepts no responsibility or liability for any loss or damage caused by the advice given in this book.

www.hardycrystalblessing.com
facebook.com/dhardyacm1

Debbie Hardy

Meditation Made Easy Using Crystals

A Guide for Using Crystals during Meditation to Heal Physical, Mental, and Emotional Issues and Deepen Spiritual Connection

Contents

I dedicate this to Tom, Katelyn, John, and Marjorie for supporting my crazy ideas, letting me follow my dreams, and always being there for me.

Sometimes you have to look back at all you have experienced to see the lessons you have learned and understand what significance those experiences have on your life today.

Introduction

Meditation has become such an important part of my life, so much so that I have become passionate about sharing my experience and helping others to find it easier to meditate in order to receive the benefits of meditation themselves. By incorporating crystals into my meditation routine, I was able to enhance my meditative state tremendously and at the same time receive healing benefits from the specific crystals I used. I not only reached a deep level of self-healing, but I also became so much more in tune with my inner and Divine guidance.

The meditative journey is just that—a *journey*. It can enhance your life in so many ways if you are open to exploring it. It is also an ongoing journey. As you will read in my story, my journey began with my physical, mental, and emotional healing with meditation, but then I began tapping into more of a spiritually focused meditation that opened up so much more than I ever had expected. More and more, new experiences and profound guidance come to me during meditation, and I see it as a continuous learning experience of self-exploration and optimum well-being. Many times after I would finish a meditation session, I would sit up and think, "Wow, did that really happen?"

I am not here to convince you of what area to focus on; that is up to you. You may find you are guided into a whole new direction without realizing it until much later. What I hope to share with you in this book is how easy it can be to meditate and achieve what you are looking for with the use of crystals in your daily meditation. I have encountered so many people suffering from so many different issues, from day-to-day stress to chronic illness, and I always ask, "Do you meditate?" I have had such a personal transformation within myself that I know everyone can achieve what he or she intends, and meditation can be such a positive channel for that. Using crystals is just an added benefit to it all.

What have you got to lose? Why not try it and see for yourself? All you have to do is devote the time and invest a small amount of money in a few crystals (although they are not required to meditate). If you are an avid meditator already and have not used crystal energy in your meditation, I invite you to try some of the following techniques during your own meditation routine. Regardless if you are new to meditation or have been meditating for years, please only use the suggestions in this book that resonate with you.

My Journey

My real journey began several years ago at the age of thirty-eight. I was under a great deal of stress and very unhappy with my job for many years. I was tired, in pain, and suffering from severe migraines and bouts of depression and anxiety. At the time, I did not realize it, but I learned much later that stress was what caused all of my issues.

One morning, I woke up in severe pain with swollen hands and feet. My body was trying to tell me something. I went to the doctor, and of course, he referred me to another, and that started the cycle of doctors. It took about a year of seeing many doctors and taking several tests before they determined that I had lupus, Raynaud's syndrome, Sjögren's syndrome, hypothyroidism, hyperlipidemia, high blood pressure and anxiety. The cycle of doctors continued for a few years, and they all prescribed me medications for the various illnesses I was diagnosed with. Most of them told me, "You will be on these medications the rest of your life." I went along with it for several years and paid the high price of medication, continual medical visits, and tests that were really not helping enough for me to see any difference in how I felt. It appeared as if I was just given a bunch of labels (diagnosis) and pills, and it seemed like a never-ending cycle that I could not get out of. I wondered, was it really going to be like this the rest of my life?

Oddly enough, some of my illnesses required me to have frequent visits to the eye doctor. By strange coincidence (or maybe not coincidence), I knew my eye doctor had a vast knowledge of lupus. So one day, I decided to talk to him about it. I told him the medications I was on and what I had been diagnosed with, and he gave me some advice that started my new direction. He said very straightforwardly that I needed to exercise, aerobic and anaerobic, and that both are extremely important. I asked myself, how could I exercise if I can hardly walk up the steps without being in pain and out of breath? But I kept listening to him. He said that I needed both types because I had to get my cardiovascular system in shape to combat the extreme fatigue I was facing. He also said I needed anaerobic exercise, weight lifting, to build new healthy cells. Now, I am no medical expert, but what he said made sense to me. He also said it is very important to stop eating processed and junk foods. He continued to tell me to eat as much healthy and organic food as I can.

So I went home, and his suggestions really struck something in me. None of my other doctors said these things to me; they just kept sending me home with more pills. Of course, we are all taught to eat right and exercise, but I guess I just needed to hear it from someone who really understood what I was going through. As hard as it was to exercise, I began walking the best I could. I would walk a block or so and increase it from there. I started eating healthier as well. Then I began to incorporate light weight lifting, and that again was not easy because I was still in a great deal of pain and very swollen, but I did it anyway. Within a few weeks, I started noticing a big difference in how I felt physically. Within a month, I was off one of my pain medications.

I continued this routine for many years and eventually got off some of the other medications I was taking. I was still under a great deal of stress and had times of depression and anxiety and a feeling of being lost. I quit the job that had me so stressed and began a new job that I was rather happy with, but I still struggled with physical issues, depression, and other issues related to long term stress. A friend of mine suggested I watch the movie *The Secret* by Rhonda Byrne, which is an in-depth discussion of the law of attraction to help me see things differently. So I did, and that was the next turning point of my healing transformation. I began practicing all the things suggested in the movie, such as visualization, positive thinking, practicing gratitude, and more. It took a lot of practice to get the negative thoughts out of my head, but eventually I got the hang of it.

Then I began meditation. I started by listening to guided-meditation recordings. Every night after work I would listen to the meditations, and within a week, I found such a deep peace within myself that I began to notice even more physical, mental, and emotional changes happening—positive changes. Reaching that state of a deep, peaceful feeling is something I do not ever remember experiencing before. I kept at it because the peacefulness really reduced the worrying in my head. I had suffered from insomnia for many years, to the point of being addicted to over-the-counter sleep aids, more medications of which did not help. The insomnia and overall stress was drastically reduced right away through meditation. I was still on several medications at this point, and I tried other holistic approaches to healing such as acupuncture and hypnotherapy, both of which were very helpful in my healing journey, but I still had some physical, emotional, and mental issues I was facing from all the prior years of stressful living.

At this point, I was also searching for what my life purpose was. I just felt lost and unsure of what to do with myself for the rest of my life. So I began asking God and the Universe, "What is my purpose?" I never considered myself a religious (the practice of following specified beliefs typically involving rituals) or spiritual (finding one owns path, concentrating on the human spirit or soul) person, although I seemed to lean toward more of the spiritual aspects for most of my life. I kept getting "explore crystals" as my answer, and that answer came to me in several different forms at different times, so it got my attention. I started researching crystals and the healing properties associated with them. I had never considered working with crystals before or using them to heal. So I got *The Crystal Bible* by Judy Hall and started reading it every night after work. I purchased all the crystals suggested in that book to help with the many issues I had been dealing with over the years, and I started using them during my meditations. I used different ones for different reasons and found an even deeper state of peace during meditation. I began meditating on my own without the guided-meditations but with the use of crystal energy. Crystal energy made it so much easier than I ever expected, plus I had the benefits of the healing properties associated with them. I was more at peace, the stress was gone, I was able to sleep without the use of sleep aides, and I felt better overall. Adding crystals to my healing routines was the next level of healing and awareness of how to self-heal.

After many of my physical, mental, and emotional issues began to heal, my meditations became more focused on spiritual guidance. I learned to communicate with my spirit guides and the Divine Source of energy. I would select crystals specifically for accessing higher realms and spirit guides for guidance and inner wisdom. I got to the point in my meditation journey that I could decide what type of meditation I wanted to focus on for the day. I could focus on physical issues that may have come up or some of the long-term ones that I still needed more healing on. Sometimes I would focus on just relaxing and being in a deep state of peace, or accessing inner or Divine guidance.

I wanted to continue my learning about crystals and various ways to incorporate them into my own self-healing, so I decided to take a crystal healing course to continue my own self-healing. I loved the course so much that I took the advanced course immediately thereafter. By then, I was an avid meditator, and I was off almost all of my medications. I had transformed my life into a much more positive journey than it had been before. I had never intended to be a "crystal healer" to help others, but after my advanced course ended, I had a desire to help others heal naturally and holistically because I had experienced so much healing on my own. I thought I could definitely help others achieve the same. So I decided to open my own healing business, and I began seeing clients and hosting workshops on how to use crystals or how to meditate with crystals. I even created several guided meditations of my own to help clients that struggled with learning how to meditate. My clients and customers were so excited for the information and healing sessions. They had wonderful results in their own personal journey. I felt I had found my purpose. I was in such a state of joy to be able to help others this way.

This journey of self-healing—and what I now see as self-discovery—has been a long journey, but I have learned so much from every moment. Stress causes so many issues for all of us, and we all react to stress in different ways. Meditation has been the easiest way for me to de-stress myself, and since I have been doing it for so long now, stress is really not a factor anymore. I feel that meditation is the key to any positive self-help that anyone can use, and meditation with crystals is even more powerful in so many ways. Looking back now, I see that I had to experience all of those things in the order that I did to get to where I am today.

I can now say I am completely off all medications. Of course, I must restate my disclaimer that I am not a medical provider or licensed physician, so I cannot and will not advise you to stop any medication you may be taking. That is between you and your physician. I would like to convince you to at least try meditation to see the possibilities of what you can achieve for yourself. I just want you to understand what I experienced by changing a few things in my life, and meditation was a huge part of that. I work with and meditate with crystals every day to continue that higher vibration of optimal health. I still use the other things I learned along the way, such as exercise, eating healthy, incorporating positive thinking, and most definitely meditation. I have been able to heal my physical, mental, and emotional bodies, plus I have also used meditation for spiritual guidance and connecting to the Divine. This is what I hope to teach you in this book.

Even though I was guided to make crystals a big part of my journey, I quickly realized that meditation is too. I speak of meditation to all my clients and friends often because I am so passionate about it. Although I do not have a physical shop or healing space any more, I do continue to offer online and personalized guided meditations.

The biggest excuses I hear for not meditating is that they cannot clear the chatter or thoughts in their head to meditate effectively, or they do not have the time to devote to it. It does take a little bit of practice to clear the chatter in your head, but I have found that using crystal energy makes it so much easier than trying to meditate without them. As far as devoting time to it, once you get into a routine and find what works best for you, you may find yourself making time for daily meditation. You do not have to devote hours upon hours a day to meditation; you can start off with just a few minutes and work your way up to a time duration that works best for you. All you have to do is have an open mind and give it the effort to try and find the time.

I believe meditation can heal so much in so many areas, so my hope for you is that you can look at your challenges and see how you can work with meditation to help you find relief for what you have been facing as well.

Chapter 1

What Is Meditation?

Before we dive into using crystals with meditation, I want to give you a foundation of what meditation is and what it can help with and then work our way from there. So we will begin with learning what meditation is, and I will offer suggestions to help make it more enjoyable overall. Meditation should not have to be a chore, something you dread or do not look forward to doing. Meditation can be an exploration of self-discovery and self-healing in so many ways, and it should be a time when you actually look forward to the experience.

There are many different definitions of meditation out there, depending on different sources you research. Some may say that meditation is spending time in quiet thought or clearing the mind for purposes of relaxation. From my practices of meditation, I have found that by clearing your mind, you are able to heal the physical, mental, and emotional issues you may be suffering from. Plus, it brings you to a deeper spiritual connection to the

Divine, which can give Divine guidance and understanding. So I would say that meditation is spending quiet time to clear your mind, to achieve relaxation, to heal the body, and to connect to Divine energy.

I feel there are no specific "rules" you need to follow to meditate. Some cultures or meditation practitioners feel you need to sit in a certain position or say specific mantras throughout the meditation, and while that is fine for some, it is not required to achieve a deep state of meditation and still receive all the benefits that meditation can provide. In the following chapters, I will explain exactly how to go about using crystals during meditation, plus I will take you through a guided meditation that you can record with your own voice and use whenever you like.

Once you get the hang of meditation and experience the benefits, you may want to find the time to meditate more often. The more you meditate, the easier it gets, and in a short amount of time, you will start to see changes physically, mentally, emotionally, and even spiritually. You can also get to the point of receiving profound inner guidance or messages that can help guide you with day-to-day activities or even problems you may have encountered. Plus, you can have a deeper connection to Spirit, God, or Creator (or whomever else you refer to as a higher power).

Focus Areas

You may be wondering what kinds of areas you can focus on for meditative healing. Although I mentioned you could focus on physical, mental, emotional, or spiritual areas for healing, it really is that open. When I began my meditation journey, I was most interested in finding a way to relieve my depression and clear my mind of worry and stress. I was able to reach such a deep state of peace and relaxation during meditation rather quickly. So my depression, among other symptoms, dissolved within days. (However, everyone is different, and everyone will respond differently.) Then I noticed my overall mood improved, and then my sleeping habits improved. So focusing on one area can actually help many other areas. Once I started experiencing the benefits, I continued meditation daily.

At the time, I was working in a rather stressful position, and oftentimes I would come home from work feeling tense, tired, upset, worried, or other heavy feelings and/or physical symptoms. I would immediately go into meditation as soon as I got home. Once I came out of the meditative state, I felt refreshed, peaceful, and relaxed, and if I was experiencing tension or pain prior to the meditation, most often that was either gone completely or quite a bit less than when I started. By noticing such a profound difference in my moods and how I felt physically after daily meditation, I decided to incorporate meditation into my daily routine.

Even to this day, I still make the time to meditate, regardless of my schedule, because it has helped me tremendously. It is that important to me to continue with it every day.

Here are some things to think about when you get started to narrow your focus when you begin your meditation journey. Of course, you can focus on one area and then move to another area depending on your own specific needs. This list is just a starting point, so if you have another specific focus, by all means, please focus on what you need to most.

- Bring clarity to a situation
- Relieve specific pain or illness in your body
- Relieve stress, worry, anxiety, or depression
- Focus on feeling more energized
- Reach a deeper connection to Divine
- Experience a deep peace within
- Be able to relax
- Become confident or release doubt
- Be open to manifest your desires
- Heal past experiences or past lives
- Strengthening relationships
- Receive inner guidance and understanding
- Overall release of negative energy

There are so many more areas that can be focused on, it really is unlimited. I have found that many of these issues can be resolved just by reaching a state of deep peace, but of course, everyone responds differently, so everyone will have different results. Once you start to see the results, you will most likely want to continue meditating.

Chapter 2

Making Meditation Easier

First, find a quiet place where you will not be disturbed for a period of time. You can sit in a comfortable chair or on the floor, lie down in your bed or on a sofa, or whatever else works for you. Some practice meditation sitting on the floor in lotus position (legs crossed with spine straight), and although that is fine for some, it is not easy or practical for everyone. Remember, there are no "rules" to meditation, and the position you meditate in is really up to you. The key here is to just get comfortable.

Once you find the place where you feel comfortable meditating, then you can add other things to enhance your experience and make it more relaxing and enjoyable. Someday you might surprise yourself and discover that you look forward to meditation. Make it your own special, sacred place. Here are some suggestions of things to try to help make meditation easier and more enjoyable for you as you begin your meditative journey. Just try what sounds good to you; you do not have to use any of the following suggestions that do not sound like something you want to try. You can try some of these and then you may decide you do not need to use them anymore at one point.

Music or Nature Sounds

You may want to incorporate music during your meditation. There are many different types of meditation music out there that are very calming and peaceful to listen to. Explore all the options; you may find you really like something such as Native American flute or drum music or Tibetan singing bowl music. Listen to a few samples of different types you had not considered before. Try to avoid popular music because you do not want the words to get stuck in your head; that defeats the purpose of clearing your mind. Spa or instrumental-type music would also be quite suitable. Consider listening to calming piano, flute, or acoustic guitar music. Some meditative music mixes instruments and nature sounds, or you can even just listen to the nature sounds too. There is a very large selection of nature sounds, such as listening to the ocean, rain, or birds chirping. Pick something that helps you feel calm and that you would love to listen to. Be sure to listen to samples of the music or nature sounds before you purchase them because you will want to be sure you like the tone and sound and see if it has a calming quality to you. If there is some part of the music or sounds you dislike, you may find yourself more annoyed during the meditation and not wanting to bother with it. This is another key factor in finding what you personally like.

Guided Meditations

You can also try guided meditations. This is a great way to start out with meditation, and there are many guided meditations out there to explore. This is where you listen while someone guides you through the complete meditation. You might find after a few times of listening to guided meditations that you will be ready to meditate without them. I began my meditative journey listening to guided meditations. I tried Dr. Brian Weiss and Esther Hicks because I found their voices ones that I could listen to easily and just follow along with the guided journey they took me on. It was not long after I began listening to guided meditations when I discovered I could follow the same format and just talk myself through similar relaxation prompts and quiet my mind on my own. If you choose to work with guided meditations, you can do so as long as you like. Again, listen to samples before you purchase one so you resonate with the person's voice. You do not want to get something that you will not like listening to. Plus, look to see what type of guided meditation journey he or she will be taking you on before you purchase one. Get an idea of the intention so it aligns with what you hope to get out of it. For example, if you are trying to attract love into your life but you purchase one that relates to something completely different, you may not be compelled to use it.

Calming Scents and Other Items

Another suggestion to help make meditation easier and more enjoyable is to burn incense or sage, or you can put a few drops of your favorite essential oils in a diffuser. You can also light some candles, bring in fresh flowers, and turn on a Himalayan salt lamp. All of these elements reduce or eliminate negative energy, so it makes your sacred space a much more calm and peaceful place.

Pillows and Blankets

Maybe you would like to use a soft blanket or eye pillow to be more comfortable. Try adding a few drops of your favorite calming essential oil to your pillow to make it even more relaxing.

Mantras

Some people like to say mantras during meditation. Mantras can be a syllable, a sound, a word, or a small grouping of words that are repeated for the duration of meditation. This is very common in many cultures during time of prayer or meditation. You can even create your own mantra that is specific to your own healing. For example, if you suffer from anxiety, you could try a mantra such as "I am calm. I am at peace" and just repeat it continually. Focus on the words and how you feel as you say them at a constant pace. It is a good way to keep your mind clear of thoughts, but it is not necessary or required. Try it if it feels right to you. There are also recorded mantras to listen to as well, so you can explore those to help you get ideas if you wish to try working with mantras.

Meditation Duration

How long should you meditate? Well, to begin, try to get at least ten minutes a day in, and then increase it from there. Once you get into a routine, your body will tell you what the right time duration will be. Some people like to meditate a few times a day or just occasionally. I suggest trying to meditate at least once a day for optimum benefits and results.

However, these are all just suggestions to help you find a relaxing atmosphere and bring a sense of calmness to you. Have fun trying the different suggestions to make it your own special experience. In the following chapters, we will discuss what crystals to use and how to use them during meditation.

Chapter 3

Choosing Crystals for Meditation

I get this question quite often. What is the best way to choose what crystals to work with? Well, I always respond, "What is it you are trying to achieve with crystals?" You can work on physical, mental, or emotional healing or spiritual development and guidance. So first, get a clear idea of what you want to accomplish using crystals during meditation. Start with one area and go from there. If you are suffering from a physical issue, choose a crystal that can help with those specific issues. For example, if you suffer from pain or inflammation, choose a crystal specific for those symptoms. If you want to reduce stress or anxiety, again, choose crystals that work well to relieve those specific symptoms. In later chapters, I will go more into detail with working with crystals for various results for healing and guidance.

A great resource for crystals is *The Crystal Bible*, by Judy Hall. She includes a comprehensive list of crystals and all the possible uses for each one in an easy-to-follow book. Look up your symptoms and see what crystals can help with those symptoms. You can order crystals online or visit your local metaphysical or crystal shop and explore crystals they have available. If you visit a local crystal shop, let your intuition guide you as to what crystals you may need at this time. You might be surprised by which ones you are drawn to right away. Look at the healing properties associated with the crystal and see if it resonates with you. Most tumbled crystals are rather inexpensive, so choose a few you are drawn to work with. Look at them, pick them up, and notice how they feel as you hold them. Sometimes you can determine if a crystal is right for you if you spend a few minutes holding it and looking at it. It will tell you if it should go home with you.

You will find that most crystals can help many areas of the physical, mental, emotional, and spiritual body. You may also find that you are very drawn to a specific crystal but it does not list the condition you wish to work on. You may want to get that crystal as well. It may be something that your intuition is telling you that you may need in the future, or it could be one you need now but the description does not quite match your symptoms. I have experienced that before as well. As you learn to work with crystals, you will find the many different ways they will help you. For example, when I first started working with crystals, I was drawn to use a small, polished labradorite. I looked up the meanings and saw the various ways to use it in healings, but I was guided to use it for pain in my upper back and neck area. That is something I could not find listed in the many resources that I checked for this specific crystal. So I decided to use it by placing it under my back and meditated with it there for several days in a row. I had wonderful results, and my pain subsided. I noticed a difference right away, and then I knew I could use that crystal for that very specific reason. Even though I could not find pain relief associated with labradorite in all my various references, I followed my intuition, and it worked out to help me. So go with what your intuition tells you when you select the crystals you want to work with. All the printed resources (and there are a lot) are a great starting point, but your body and the crystals know which ones you ultimately need.

If you are still unsure of what crystals to begin with, here are a few suggestions for any starting point. I am not going to get too much into the meanings of crystals here because there are so many resources on crystal meanings and healing properties already out there (check out *The Crystal Bible* by Judy Hall or *The Book of Stones* by Robert Simmons and Naisha Ahsian).

Clear Quartz

Most everyone working with crystals should have a clear quartz. Quite oftentimes it is clear but can be a milky-white hue as well. It is the ultimate healer of anything and provides an abundance of positive energy. It also amplifies energy, so if you use it with another crystal, it will amplify the healing properties of that other crystal. It is attuned to work with the person needing energy healing and will work for specific areas of the healing. It works well for all chakra points (chakras are energy wheels located around the aura of the physical body) and healing of mental, spiritual, and emotional levels, plus it can bring you to a deeper spiritual connection.

Amethyst

The second choice I would suggest is amethyst, which can be a dark or light purple color. This is such a peaceful crystal, and it will bring a peaceful calmness to a space or person. It is highly protective of the person working with it. It is associated with the third-eye chakra and crown chakra, so it will assist with developing intuition and having an overall sense of Divine connection. Because of its calming and peaceful energy, this is an excellent choice of crystal to place by your bed or under your pillow for help with insomnia.

Rose Quartz

The third crystal I would recommend is rose quartz, which can be a very light pink to a darker pink color. This is a very loving crystal. It brings love to a person and helps facilitate self-love as well. It can also assist with the grieving process, forgiveness of self and others, and finding compassion in a situation.

There are thousands of crystals to work with. Usually the best way to choose the crystals that can help you is by using your intuition and examining what you are drawn to at first sight. Plus remember, you can do some research on the symptoms or issues you may be facing and choose crystals based on that. In the following chapters, you will learn how to meditate with crystals, and you will learn the actual guidelines I provide for meditation.

Chapter 4

Meditation with Crystals

Select Items to Use During Meditation

First of all, gather all the items you will be using, such as music or guided meditations, incense or essential oils, or possibly an eye pillow. Remember, these are just suggestions, so try what feels right to you.

Get Comfortable

Then select the crystal(s) you wish to work with. You can sit or lie down during your meditation. Some prefer to sit in lotus position, crossed legs with spine straight; others prefer to sit in a comfortable chair, or you can find a comfortable place to lie down. Remember, there are no rules to meditation, so choose what suits you best.

One of the key components of meditation is being comfortable, so find the place where you will be comfortable for your meditation session.

Hold Crystal(s)

To begin using crystals during meditation, hold your crystal in your receptive hand; this would be your nondominant hand. You can experiment with adding more crystals or just using one. If you add more crystals, you can hold one in each hand, place them on certain points of your body, or place them around your body.

Relaxation Process

Once you find that comfortable place, hold your crystal, close your eyes, and take three deep breaths. In and out. Fill your lungs completely with a deep breath in, and when you exhale, release any tension, stress, or worry you have been holding on to. Do this three times, and then let your breathing go natural, nice and steady easy breathing. Next, focus on relaxing your whole body. Start at your toes and work your way up to the top of your head. Visualize yourself relaxing. Start by relaxing your toes and feet and then relax your legs and thighs. During this time, keep breathing nice, steady breaths, and then relax your hips and core area and then your chest and shoulders. Remember to keep breathing nice and steady, and relax your arms, hands, and fingers.

Then relax your neck and forehead, your jaw and mouth. Just breathe nice and easy and relax completely.

Focus on Breath and Crystal Energy

When you reach the state of relaxation, just focus on your breath going in and out, in and out. Also, focus on the crystal you are holding. Feel its energy in your hand. The more you work with crystals, the more you will feel their energy. Eventually you will begin to feel the energy go up your arm and even surround your whole body. It can feel like a tingling or a wave of energy swirling around you. You may also experience a cool or warm sensation. By focusing on the energy from the crystal, you are less likely to remember to think day-to-day thoughts. You have a focal point with crystal energy. If day-to-day thoughts enter your mind, just acknowledge them and let them go, and then refocus on your breathing, in and out, and the crystal in your hand. This may take a bit of practice, but holding the crystal and feeling its energy makes it much easier to meditate. Plus, as an added bonus, you get the healing benefits from the crystal at the same time.

Visions and Colors

Some people, but not all, experience seeing visions and various colors during meditation using crystals. This is actually quite common. You may experience a vision similarly to what it would be like when you dream. The visions can be symbols or scenarios that may mean something to you presently or in the future. You may also experience seeing colors while you are in the meditative state. You may see the color of the crystal you are holding surround you or even something completely different. Different crystals may cause more visions or colors to appear than other crystals. Just be open to what comes to you and enjoy the experience.

Everyone learns to meditate at a different rate. Do not give up if it is taking you a bit longer than expected. Even if you meditate for just a few minutes a day, that is a starting point, and you will still receive the benefits of meditation from that short duration of time. You may begin to increase your time without realizing it, and it should become easier to achieve. Some days it can be even harder to focus on meditation than others are, but that is part of the learning process. Plus, some days you might just want to clear and quiet your mind and find peace without any other specific reason to meditate. Oftentimes, I would come home after a stressful day at work, go straight to my room, and meditate. I would grab my favorite crystals, turn off the light, and just start focusing on my breathing and the energy of the crystals I was holding. Every time I do this after a stressful day or occurrence, I come out of the meditation feeling light, refreshed, and more at peace than I was when I began. That in itself is such a healing experience. Bringing yourself back to peace and calm after a stressful day combats all the negative reactions your body goes through while under stress.

The more and more you meditate, you may find yourself focusing your attention on specific intentions for the meditation. You can have the intention to just find that peaceful state of calmness after a stressful moment or day. Or you can focus on a very specific area you want to heal. Plus, there are times you may have the intention of wanting to connect to your higher self or spirit guides for guidance or wisdom on a certain situation you are experiencing. Whatever reason you choose, it is all beneficial. Just clearing the day-to-day thoughts from your mind and bringing your body, mind, and spirit to a state of peace are such wonderful feelings. You may find that you will want to meditate more often because it does make you feel better overall.

Chapter 5

Guided Meditation

Here is a guided meditation that you can record with your own voice so you can listen to it any time you like. This meditation is to guide you to release all energies that no longer serve you. You can use it to focus on releasing pain, stress, sadness, anger, financial blocks, relationship issues or anything else you may want to release. I find this very helpful when going through a challenging time or experiencing a huge change that is difficult to deal with. You can also use it for day to day issues that may arise.

Begin by getting comfortable in your quiet space. Then select a crystal you wish to work with that aligns with what you want to focus on. Hold your crystal and use any of the tips or suggestions from chapter 2 that resonate with you. The words in italics can be recorded to create your own guided meditation. Pace yourself to give yourself some time, and use the ellipses to take a moment or pause before recording the next sentence. Practice it a few times before you record it so you can get a feel for how fast you go through the prompts. It would be ideal if this ended up being about a twenty-minute recording.

Let's begin by closing your eyes and taking three deep breaths in and out...
Inhale a deep, cleansing breath...Fill your lungs completely...
Exhale all stress or worry of the day...
Inhale another deep, healing, cleansing breath...
Exhale all concerns that are holding you back...
Inhale one more deep, healing, cleansing breath...
Exhale all that no longer serves you...

Now, just let your breathing go natural, nice, easy, and steady...

Let's focus on relaxing your whole body...
Begin by relaxing your toes, feet, and ankles...
Relax your knees and legs...
Relax your thighs and hips...
Keep breathing nice and easy...
Relax your core area and stomach...
Relax your chest and shoulders...
Relax your arms, hands, and fingers...
Just breathe nice and easy...
Relax your neck and forehead...
Relax your eyes, mouth, and jaw...
Just relax completely and let everything else go...

Next, visualize a white, radiant light surrounding your whole body in a bubble of light. This is a Universal light that is very healing and protective. You are protected in this beautiful white light.

Now visualize a staircase with ten steps going down...
With each step I count down, you will be more relaxed...
Ten...
Nine...
Eight...
Seven...
More and more relaxed...
Six...
Five...
Four...
Even more relaxed...
Three...
Two...
One...

Now you see a door in front of you...When you are ready, go to the door and open it...
Walk through the door...and in the distance, you see a small fire burning in a circle ...Start walking toward the fire. Remember, you are safe in this place...Take as much time as you need to get to the fire...and as you walk toward the fire, notice your surroundings...Is it daylight or night?...

Are there others around, or is it just you?...
As you continue your journey, notice if you are in a field, on a beach, in the mountains, or somewhere else...
Is the fire on a rock, in the dirt, or in a fire pit of some kind?...
Keep walking toward the fire and keep noticing the details that surround you...
Remember, you are safe in this place...
Do you see any animals?...
Trees?...
Flowers or bushes?...
Do you hear any sounds?...
Remember, you are in a safe place, so you can continue your journey...
Once you reach the fire, you see a bowl of sage leaves at your feet...
Sage is very healing and cleansing...
You may sit by the fire or continue to stand; the choice is yours...
Pick up the bowl of sage leaves and throw a piece of sage in the fire for each thing that you wish to release...

Take a moment and think about what you want to release...

It could be pain...worry...stress...illness...fear...anger...sadness ...judgement...negative thoughts, or a combination of those...or something else...

One at a time, throw a sage leaf in the fire for everything you wish to release...

Feel the release happening within your body...

Feel yourself becoming lighter and less burdened...

Continue throwing sage leaves into the fire for all you wish to release...

Take your time with this process...

Once you have finished releasing...just take a moment to reflect on how you feel...Notice if you feel lighter...less pain...more at peace...or something else...

Look into the fire and just let it all go...Feel the complete release of all negative energies being dissolved in the fire and going up with the smoke of the sage leaves...up to the Universe...

Now, give thanks for the release...
You can stay in this place as long as you like and just continue to notice how well you feel...(pause a bit longer here)
When you are ready to return, turn around and continue your journey back to the door from which you came...You can take as long as you need as you walk back to the door...

As you walk back to the door, keep noticing how good you feel...
How light and free you feel...
How at peace you feel...
Once you get to the door, go through the door...
And start walking your way back up the steps...
As we count our way up the steps, you will feel more and more alert and conscious of your environment...
One...
Two...
Three...
Four...
More and more alert...
Five...
Six...
Seven...
Eight...
Almost there...
Nine...
Ten...

Take a deep breath...Wiggle your fingers and toes...
And when you are ready, open your eyes.

You can spend as much or little time at the prompts as you like. If part of the meditation does not resonate with you, change it to suit your preferences. This is provided for you to help you get the feel for meditation and assist you with your meditation journey.

Chapter 6

Journaling Your Experience

I always suggest to journal your meditations, especially when you first start out. It is a good way to monitor your progress on how it is helping in the various areas of your life, but you can also record information about the crystals you work with during meditation. You never know what kind of insights or information may come through during or after meditation that you may want to remember or refer back to later, so this is a great way to do that.

Quite oftentimes, I would journal my meditation experiences and then go back and refer to it at a later date because something else came up that seemed related in some way and maybe there was a connection to what was in the meditation.

Select a journal that is just for meditation and thoughts that come from mediation. Make it your own special meditation journal. You can decorate it or keep it simple. Keep it in a special place near where you meditate so you can access it right after meditation.

Journal Before Meditation

Begin by entering the date and what crystal you decided to work with. Write down everything you feel prior to the meditation—mentally, emotionally, and physically. For example, do you feel tired and frustrated? Is there pain or other physical issues in an area of your body? Do you feel sad and hopeless? Are you happy and content? Whatever you are experiencing at that moment, write it in your journal. If you are suffering from pain, gauge how severe that pain is from one to ten, with ten being highest, and record that in your journal. If you feel tired, gauge that from one to ten, and anything else you are experiencing record in your journal.

If you are using a new crystal, it is a good idea to journal the experiences you have with the crystal as well. Before your meditation, write in your journal what type of crystal you chose to work with. It is usually a good idea to meditate with a new crystal for at least three to five days to get a feel for how it reacts to you and how you react to it to notice if it has helped you in some way.

By journaling this information, you can always refer back to it in case you forget what crystals helped you with certain areas.

Then begin your meditation. Hold your crystal and go through your breathing and relaxation phases and try to meditate for as long as you can.

Journal After Meditation

When you are finished with your meditation, journal your experience in as much detail as you can, plus write down the duration of the time you were in meditation. You will probably see that your time duration increases rather quickly and then level out at some point. Write down how you feel after the meditation. If you had pain or other specific issues before the meditation, gauge yourself again and see if the numbers went down. For example, if you gauged your pain at a level of seven before the meditation, gauge it again after the meditation and see if the number dropped. Sometimes it can drop immediately, and sometimes it can take a few days to notice a difference. Do this with emotional and mental issues you may have recorded in your journal as well. Journal how you feel overall after the meditation. Do you feel less stress or less worry? Do you feel more at peace? Do you notice if you are more energized or alert? Some people notice these changes right away, but for others, it can be a few days. Do not get discouraged or give up. You took the first step and that was the hardest. Next, journal what you experienced during the meditation. Did you feel any physical sensations, such as warm or cold, tingling, or an overall sense of energy flowing around you? Did you notice any emotional sensations come about? Sometimes those need to release during or after meditation. That is part of the healing process.

Also, journal how the crystal felt in your hand; did you feel the energy? If so, was the energy just felt in your hand or did you feel the energy go up your arm or to other areas of your body? If not, you just may need to get used to its energy, and eventually you should begin to feel something from it. You will start to get a sense of what crystals you will want to work with for the different healing energies they provide specifically for you. Plus, journal if you struggled with day-to-day thoughts or if you were able to quiet your mind. Journaling all this information is a good way to refer back to see your progress. Of course, it is not required to journal; it is just a good way to track your progress in different areas.

After five days of meditation, refer back to day one and see if you notice any significant changes in how you feel or how the crystal has responded during meditation. For example, if you chose a crystal to help you communicate more effectively then look back and determine if you noticed a positive change in your communication skills. Do you think it has helped? How do you feel overall physically, mentally, and emotionally? Do you find yourself sleeping better at night? Do you feel less stressed or anxious? Do you feel more peace and calm? Do you feel more focused during the day? Eventually, once you get the hang of meditation, you can also meditate for spiritual and Divine guidance, so I suggest that you journal any messages you receive during those sessions as well. Sometimes you may notice results within a day or so, while other times it may take several days to notice changes. It depends on what issues you are trying to resolve and the severity of the issue. If you did not notice any changes at all after the five days, then try a different crystal or try other music or essential oils (or any of the other suggestions listed in chapter 2) until you find the right fit for you.

Here is a basic guideline for journaling your experience. Feel free to use this format in your own journal or create your own format. It does not have to be formal journal writing; the purpose is to document what you have learned from the session before, during, and after and the days following your initial meditation. Plus, it is helpful to document how you respond to different crystals because some crystals may react to your body more so than other crystals do.

Basic Guideline Meditative Journal Worksheet

Date   Crystal(s) used

Journal how you feel before the session physically, mentally, and emotionally. Remember to gauge your symptoms so you can determine if there were any improvements after the session.

You can use this scale to gauge your main symptoms if you are focusing on reducing a specific symptom. Gauge the symptom from one to ten, ten being the highest, and circle that number on the scale below.

Symptom Scale—premeditation

Symptom_____

1   2   3   4   5   6   7   8   9   10

Journal how you feel physically, mentally, and emotionally immediately following the session. Also enter any insights, visions, colors, physical energy, or feelings that you may have noticed during the session. Gauge your prior symptoms at this time to see if there were any improvements.

Symptom Scale—postmeditation

1   2   3   4   5   6   7   8   9   10
After a few days of meditation with the same crystal, journal any differences or improvements you may have noticed overall. Also journal any insights that may come to you in the next few days. Plus you may want to record if you felt if the crystal you worked with was effective for the intention you used it for.

Chapter 7

Five-Minute Quick Meditation

There may be times when you need a quick boost or a quick de-stressing, but you just do not have the time to dedicate to going into a full meditation. These quick five-minute mini meditations are a perfect solution for that, and they can be done anytime and anywhere. You can go sit in your car (please do not do this while you are driving), in a restroom, outside somewhere, or even at your desk at work. Try it somewhere where you will not be interrupted by phones or conversation for a few minutes.

When I worked a nine-to-five job, I had a dish of tumbled crystals on my desk for that very reason. If I began to experience fatigue or stress, I would hold on to the appropriate crystal for the issue I wanted to resolve for the five-minute crystal mini meditation and afterward would feel like I could continue on my day productively. Once you get used to what crystals help you with certain issues, you may find your own personal selection in various places in your home, office, or purse. Place the ones you would want to use most in an easy-to-get-to place so you can access them immediately when needed. Here are a few that would be good to have on hand for a quick five-minute hold.

- Amethyst to reduce stress
- Moonstone to reduce stress
- Carnelian to increase energy
- Fluorite to increase clarity
- Citrine to increase joy
- Clear quartz to increase positive energy
- Black tourmaline to reduce negative energy

If you have certain other favorite crystals to work with, you can create your own little custom stash or dish to have on hand.

To do the five-minute crystal mini meditation, hold your selected crystal in your receptive hand (your nondominant hand) and close your eyes. Just focus on the energy of the crystal in your hand. Take a few deep breaths in through your nose and exhale through your mouth. Then just let your breathing go natural and easy. Visualize the color of the crystal you are holding surrounding you in a bubble of light as you continue to hold the crystal. For example, if you are holding an orange-colored crystal, visualize an orange bubble of light surrounding your body. Continue to do this for about five minutes and then open your eyes. Then take a few sips of water if you can. Compare how you felt when you started to how you feel after the five minute quick hold meditation.

Here are a few scenarios in which the five-minute quick meditation can be used.

Fatigued or Tired

If you start to feel fatigued during your day and need a boost of energy to get you through the rest of the day, select your favorite orange crystal. It can be a carnelian, orange calcite, tigereye, mookaite, sunstone, or any other orange crystal you may have. Any of those would work fine. If you have a severe case of fatigue, try this technique for ten minutes. However, I have found that generally five minutes usually does the trick. After the five minute quick mini meditation, check your energy levels. Do you feel as if you can move on with your day more energetically than before the mini meditation? Do you feel as if you have more zest and energy overall? I have replaced the afternoon candy-and-coffee routine with this, and it has been very successful for me. Give it a try.

Stressed or Anxious

If you begin to feel stressed or anxious for any reason, hold a moonstone, amethyst, rose quartz, or any other crystal that makes you feel calm. Follow the same procedure described above, and if you need to increase the time duration, please do so. You should be able to gauge the results on how tense your muscles are before and after. See if you are breathing normally instead of erratically. Do your emotions feel more stable? Are you able to think clearly and in a calm manner? I would use the calming crystals when an immediate change happened, if I had a big project that I was working on, or if I was approaching a deadline and I was feeling a bit frazzled.

Organization and Focus

If you are working on a project and it requires organization and deep focus to accomplish, then use a fluorite, lepidolite, or jasper crystal. A good way to gauge how you are feeling after the five-minute meditation with one of these crystals is to see if you can think clearly again. Do you have a sense of organization that you did not have a few minutes ago? Do you have a new sense of wanting to accomplish the task than you did before the meditation?

You can also get a feel for the crystal's energy by using the five-minute quick mini meditation. This works well if you get a new crystal that you want to see what kind of immediate energy you feel with it. Just try a five-minute mini meditation with any crystal you may have or want to work with to determine if you can feel its energy or if you react to it in any way. This is also a good process to follow to learn to get a feel for crystal energy overall.

Chapter 8

Meditation for Physical, Emotional, and Mental Healing

Physical Healing by Meditating with Crystals

There are many different crystals to work with for physical healing. You will have to decide what area of physical healing you want to start with. (For instance, if you suffer from headaches, choose an appropriate crystal that has the healing properties to help relieve headaches.) Here are just a few suggestions, but the areas of focus are endless. You can focus on pain management, healing a specific illness, reducing inflammation, reducing stomach or digestive issues, increasing your immune system support, relieving insomnia, reducing allergies, and PMS or menopausal support. You can even focus on overall health and well-being. Do some research on what crystals can help the physical area that you want to focus on.

The Crystal Bible by Judy Hall and *The Book of Stones* by Robert Simmons and Naisha Ahsian are excellent resources for the various uses of crystal energy. Some crystals to start off could be bloodstone for detoxifying the body, moss agate to strengthen the immune system, carnelian to bring energy to you, malachite or hematite for pain and inflammation relief, peach selenite to help with female issues such as PMS or menopausal symptoms, or clear quartz for use with any area of healing. There are so many more for these issues and other issues you may be facing, so choose the crystals that you feel you need most. Once you have the crystal(s) you want to work with, there are a few different ways you can use them.

I have worked with many different crystals to help the many different issues I had been dealing with over the years. So start with one issue to focus on and then go from there. Do not try to heal everything at once. Although I am sure it has happened before, I think it is more realistic to focus on what is the most important area you want support in at that point in time. Once you begin to feel relief in that specific area, then move on to another area. I began my healing journey focusing on reducing stress, anxiety, and depression, and by doing so, many physical symptoms began to heal as well. Once I began noticing relief in the stress area, then I moved on to other areas to focus on.

First, you can place the crystal on the area of the body that needs support. For example, if you suffer from pain in your hip, you can place the crystal you selected on your hip for a period of time. You can sit or lie down quietly for ten to fifteen minutes with the crystal placed on your body, and as you do, visualize the pain lifting off your body or dissolving away. Focus your attention on the energy and vibration the crystal gives you and remember to breathe. Or you can follow the guidelines mentioned in the previous chapters of fully meditating with the selected crystal. You can surround your body with the selected crystals, place them on your body, or just hold them during meditation. Visualize the color of light (the same color of the crystal) surrounding your body and reducing or eliminating the pain (or other physical issue you are focusing on healing) while doing so.

You can use more than one type of crystal to achieve this, and several of the same type of crystal but I would not suggest more than four different types at a time. If you use too many different types of crystals, the energies can get confused and may not be as effective.

Mental and Emotional Healing

If you are focusing on mental and/or emotional healing, you can use the same guidelines, such as holding an appropriate crystal or placing several beside your body for a period of time or meditating with them. Again, you will want to find the crystals that correspond to the issues you are facing. Some suggested crystals to begin with for mental or emotional healing could be fluorite to bring you clarity of mind, citrine to bring joy, moonstone to bring calmness, amethyst to bring peace, rose quartz to bring love and/or forgiveness, and clear quartz to bring in positive energy. Try to choose specific crystals for specific issues you are dealing with.

Releasing & Receiving Crystal Layout

When I was suffering because I could not find peace within myself from past events from my childhood, I was given a crystal layout by my spirit guides to help me try to release any past wounds that I may have been holding onto. I am going to share that crystal layout with you so you can try it for yourself. I call this layout the releasing and receiving crystal layout because we focus on releasing the negative energy and then we receive positive energy. A crystal layout is specific crystals placed around the body with the intention for a specific outcome. I find this layout helpful if you are suffering from depression, anxiety, worry, or stress. It can actually be used for most any physical, emotional, or mental issue, but I found it quite useful for my emotional and mental issues I was trying to resolve at the time. After one meditative session with this layout, I was relieved of my distress and was able to move on from the situation. I have used this specific layout on several clients, and some have responded quickly as well while others had to use it a few times. It depends on the severity of the issues you are trying to resolve, but I found it effective in many cases.

Of course, I have to say that this does not replace medical or psychological care, and if you need the care of a physician, please do so. Please refer back to the disclaimer at the beginning of the book for full disclosure.

Supplies for Layout

The layout incorporates the use of many clear quartz and one rose quartz. Clear quartz is the ultimate healer and brings in an abundance of positive energy. I was guided to use clear quartz points because they can work two ways. First, we focus on drawing out negative energy and then replace it by bringing in positive energy, and the clear quartz points are perfect for that process. You will need approximately fifteen to twenty one- to two-inch clear quartz points. They can be rough, unpolished, natural points, and in most cases, you can find them rather inexpensively. You will also need a tumbled rose quartz crystal and a small bundle of sage. If you do not like the smoke of sage or cannot handle the smoke of sage, you can use sage essential oil in a diffuser or sage spray as an alternative. Other suitable alternative choices are frankincense, Palo Santo, peppermint, myrrh or cedarwood; however, I recommend sage for optimal results. If you are using essential oil in a diffuser, you can have that on for the duration of the process, but the sage smudge or spray will be used at the midway point of the meditation. You can have someone assist you with the placement of the crystals and sage cleansing segment but it is something that can be achieved alone as well.

Clear Crystal Energy

Once you get your crystals, clear their energy by holding them under running water for a moment to cleanse any energy that may have been absorbed from others touching them prior to your use. After this session, you will want to cleanse them again.

Before you begin, just be aware that this crystal layout meditation may bring up certain emotions that need to be released.

Phase 1 of Layout

To do this meditation, you will want to lie down in a comfortable place where you will not be disturbed for twenty to thirty minutes. Place the twenty clear points all around your body (as shown in diagram 1) with the points pointing away from your body. This will bring out the negative energy. Then place the rose quartz at your heart center and place your arms to your sides. Begin by focusing on your breathing and relaxing as we discussed in chapter 4.

Then start mentally scanning your body for any negative feelings and just start visualizing all negative energies releasing from your body. Take as much time as you need to do this process. Some may visualize it as being dark clouds drifting away, some may feel energy exit their hands or legs, some may just feel a heaviness lifting off of them, and some may not feel or visualize anything at all. The key here is to just focus on releasing all negative energies from your being. If it helps, you can even repeat a mantra quietly to yourself, such as "I release all negative energies...I release all negative energies." Once you start to feel rather relaxed and good, then do one last mental scan of your body to see if there are any lingering mental, emotional, or physical traces of tension anywhere and release the energy causing that too. This initial process can take from fifteen to twenty minutes, depending on the severity of the issue you are trying to resolve.

Phase 2 of Layout

When you feel that the negative energy has left your body, then cleanse the points by sage smudging them. You can sit up to do this part of the process, but try not to move around too much. So sit up, light your sage smudge bundle (be fire safe of course), and sage smudge all the crystals that are around you, going in a clockwise manner. So in other words, leave all the crystals in place from the first phase of the process. Go in a clockwise manner around your body near the crystals using the smudge or spray. State something such as "I release all negative energy in this space" while you smudge the crystals around you. This way you are cleansing the crystals and your aura at the same time of any lingering negative residue. If you are using a sage spray, just spray in a clockwise manner and state your intention. You will not want to spend a lot of time with the sage smudge process because it interrupts the flow of the overall process, so just take a minute or two to do this. If you need assistance with this part of the process you can have someone do this for you while you wait quietly. After you have cleansed the crystals and aura for a few moments, then you can extinguish the sage bundle and go on to the next phase of the meditation. You may want to have a small cup of water or an abalone shell nearby to extinguish the sage bundle properly and completely.

Phase 3 of Layout

Now point all the clear quartz crystal points inward toward your body to bring in the positive energy. Lie down again and hold the rose quartz at your heart center (see diagram 2). Now begin by visualizing positive energy coming to you, entering your being. Notice how good the energy feels around you and visualize being surrounded in a bright white-and-yellow light. This is a Universal healing light that is positive and pure. So for the next ten to fifteen minutes or so, continue bringing in and filling your aura with positive energy. If you feel a little dizzy, you may need to do a little grounding once you complete this phase of the process (see chapter 11 on grounding).

Once you have finished this process, gauge how you feel compared to when you started. Do you feel lighter or happier? Do you feel more at peace or relaxed? Do you not feel any change at all? Gauge how you feel after the session to decide if you think you may need to repeat the process again or not. This can be used occasionally or often. However, give yourself a few days to adjust to the shift in energy and allow your body to rest if you decide to do it often. Just remember that everyone responds differently, so everyone will have a unique and different experience and results.

Diagram number 1: Release Negative Energy

Place the clear quartz points facing away from the body and a rose quartz tumbled stone at the heart center.

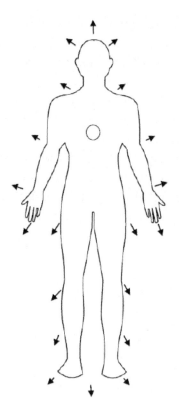

Shutterstock Licensed Modified Image

Diagram number 2: Bring in Positive Energy

Place the clear quartz points facing toward the body and a rose quartz tumbled stone at the heart center.

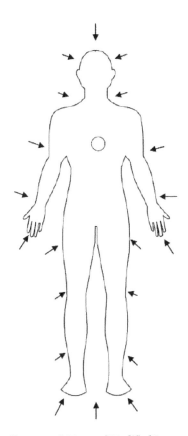

Shutterstock Licensed Modified Image

Chapter 9

Spiritual Connection Meditation

When I began my meditative journey, I was mostly focused on healing my physical, mental, and emotional issues. At that time, I had no idea that I could connect so deeply spiritually. I was on my own spiritual path, and I found that I was able to connect to Source energy, spirit guides, past lives, and other realms easily by meditating with crystals and focusing on connecting more spiritually. This, of course, did not happen overnight. I was well into my meditative journey for some time before I began to tap into this new spiritual world and insight. If spiritual connection meditation is your main objective with meditation, you may be able to access the spiritual connections much faster than I did.

About a year after I began meditating, I had really become curious as to my spiritual path. By this time, I had already incorporated crystals into my meditations, so I was well aware of the benefits crystals could provide during meditation. I had gone to a channeling session with a medium, and she said she saw my angel beside me. That had me excited! I have always believed in angels, but I never really thought about my own angel. The medium would not give me her name and said I had to figure that out myself. Since I was already meditating on a regular basis, I figured I would meditate to find my angel's name. I researched and selected crystals that were associated with connecting to angels, so I used angelite, opalite, and selenite. I began meditating with those crystals with the intent of connecting to my angel. I meditated with this intention for several weeks before I received any type of messages regarding my angel, but I was determined.

One day about five or six weeks later during meditation, the name Sarah came to me, and I asked, "Is that your name?" I was not feeling that was the correct name, but I felt it was close. I did not get an immediate response, so I kept meditating, trying to get my angel's name. At this point, I did feel an energy visiting me during the meditations. It was a soft, kind, and compassionate energy. Then a few weeks later, another name came to me, Sari. I was intrigued and curious about that name, and I asked during the meditation, "Is that your name?" and the answer came to me as a whisper "yes." I got her name! I was so excited. I had never heard of that name before, so after the meditation, I Googled it because, of course, you can find everything on Google, right? After a bit of research, I found out that Sari is a form of the name Sarah. I was in awe. I could not believe it. Since then I have been able to connect to my angel and ask and receive guidance every single time during meditation with that intention. I have even gotten to the point of connecting to her without being in the state of meditation. I have also learned to channel, experience teleporting, recall past lives, go back to heal past lives and associated karma, see future lives, connect to other realms, and connect to Source energy and other spirit guides, all while under the meditative state using crystals aligned with such intentions. Now I have a whole team of spirit guides that I consult with during meditation, and you can too.

There really is no limit to what you can accomplish during meditation, so if connecting spiritually or deepening your spiritual path and want guidance is something you are interested in, then meditation with crystals is a good way to begin.

Connecting to your guardian angel is a good way to start out if you are on your spiritual path and wish to receive more profound guidance. Of course, I would suggest you meditate with the same crystals that I tried because they are easy to find and inexpensive (angelite, opalite, and selenite). Opalite is a manufactured crystal; however, I have found it complements the energy of the other two crystals quite nicely. I still use these three crystals quite often during my meditations. Other crystals you can try are celestite, aphophylite, aurora, danburite, or rainbow quartz but these are a bit more expensive. They are higher-vibrational crystals, so you would most likely only need one of them to achieve connecting to your angel. There are many more out there, so experiment with them and see what helps you connect easily. I have used all of these crystals and found they work very well to connect to the angelic and other realms quickly. Some of my friends and clients have used these techniques when trying to connect to their guarding angel, and they have come up with their angel's name much faster than I did. If you do not get it right away, do not give up because once you get to that point you will find a whole new world opened up to you.

Connect to Guardian Angel

If you want to try to connect to your guardian angel, hold an angelite in one hand, an opalite in the other, and set the selenite on your chest or beside the midsection of your body. You will actually be guided to what works best for you after a bit of experimenting with them. Ask your angel to surround you in protective, loving, white light so only positive and pure energy comes to you during your meditation session. I do this often myself. Go through the regular relaxation techniques discussed earlier and focus on your breathing and the feel of the energy of the crystals you are holding. You may notice a very nice energy vibration from the combination of these crystals. As you focus on your breathing and the energy from the crystals, hold the intent to connect to your guardian angel and ask for her or his name. You may experience a sensation of colors or an energy surrounding you. You may also hear voices or see visions. Pay attention and be open to what happens. When I first started connecting to my angel, I visually saw an energy visiting me; it was just a form of energy. She did not appear to me (and never has) looking like an angel the way we portray them. But everyone sees and experiences it differently, so just be aware of what you feel during the meditative session.

I also recommend journaling these sessions because you may receive insight or guidance along the way that may not make sense the day of your meditation, but sometime in the future, it might correlate with something you are going through.

Once you start with meditation on a spiritual level, you can really connect and learn so much. I continue to receive daily guidance from my spirit guides, and quite oftentimes I meet new spirit guides along the way. If a new spirit guide comes to you during meditation, just ask him or her who he or she is and follow the process as mentioned above.

Chapter 10

Going Deeper into Meditation with Crystals

When I experienced connecting to my angel and spirit guides during meditation, I was truly hooked. I look forward to meditation every day to see what happens next. I had read about some very high-vibration crystals; these are crystals that Katrina Raphaell calls master crystals in her book *The Crystalline Transmission: A Synthesis of Light*. I purchased some of the crystals she mentioned in her book because I wanted to take my meditative journey even deeper than I had ever accessed before.

Working with master crystals or higher-vibration crystals can bring you to a deeper state of meditation quickly. Plus, you may feel their energy is much more prominent than that of the mainstream crystals typically used.

Cathedral Lightbrary

The first master crystal I began to work with was a Cathedral Lightbrary crystal. Katrina Raphaell describes this crystal as being a place of God (cathedral) and knowledge (library of light). In her book, she mentioned that this crystal could connect to the akashic records and past lives. I was doing a lot of past-life work at the time, and I wanted a crystal to help me access that information quicker than my regular meditative practice. By my own personal meditation with this crystal, I learned what it truly was capable of, and I saw the same vision time and time again of the hall of records in a grand cathedral. During meditations with this crystal, I would ask questions about certain things I was experiencing at the time, and I would see or receive insight in the forms of words, numbers, or just a knowing of the answer.

I also facilitated group meditations in my crystal shop with this specific crystal, and most participants would receive some insight to what they needed to know at the time. I guided the group into a relaxed state and took them to the cathedral by way of visualization during the meditation. Then I let them have a quiet time to mentally ask the questions they wish to have answers to. Most times during this group meditation, I saw many of the participants in my visions going through what looked like a library with rows after rows of books. Every person has their own book of records. Then I would see them selecting their own book or reading their own book in a quiet space. One time, one participant and I saw the exact same vision. I would always ask the group what they experienced after the meditation, and most everyone reported some sort of guidance, direction, or answer to what they asked about. So if you are interested in taking your meditative journey to access a deeper state of information or past lives, this is a wonderful crystal to work with.

If you would like to meditate with a Cathedral Lightbrary crystal, hold it in one hand or place it beside your body. Go through your relaxation techniques and clear your mind. You will most likely feel the vibration of the crystal rather quickly. Then just be open to receiving information and begin to ask questions on past lives, current life, or future lives to help you with your current life situations. Be aware of your journey to the library in the cathedral. You may find it to be a very beautiful journey, so pay attention to the details during your meditation. You may see visions or colors, hear voices or sounds, or just receive an inner knowingness. I would suggest you journal your experiences when you use this crystal during meditation.

Elestial

I also suggest using an elestial crystal if you are interested in working with past-life recall or soul connection. This is another higher-vibration master crystal mentioned in Katrina Raphaell's book, *The Crystalline Transmission*. You can meditate with this alone or with someone to find a soul connection or past-life connection between each other. If you decide to use this by yourself, you can just hold it in your receptive hand with the intent to find what past life you need to access at the moment or what you want to connect with on a soul level. It could be soul purpose, soul wisdom, or soul healing; it is really unlimited in that area.

If you decide to use an elestial with a friend or loved one during meditation, then you would meditate with it together at the same time to find your soul connection or a past-life connection. Sit facing each other or side by side, close your eyes, and follow the same relaxation techniques to clear your mind. Then focus on the intent to find your soul connection or past-life connection and be open to what information comes to you. After the meditation, you can compare the information that each of you received. You may experience or receive similar information or something completely different. However, it is still a connection and may start to make sense after you do this a few times.

I meditated with an elestial quite often with several friends, and we were successful in obtaining some very interesting information each time. During several sessions with one friend of mine, we were able to see a complete past-life journey that we had been on together. Each time we meditated with the elestial, we were able to pick up where we left off on the past-life journey until we reached the end. It was quite exciting and fun to experience such an adventure. Plus, it actually gave us some insight as to what we were experiencing in our current lives at the time.

Devic Temple

Another master crystal that I learned of from Katrina Raphaell is the devic temple crystal. The devic crystal is a high-vibration master crystal that I had purchased, and at the time, I did not even know exactly what it was I had. Katrina Raphaell describes the devic realm as "beings that exist in the higher astral and/or heaven worlds." These are beings that come to provide guidance without being personal. They are not our own personal "spirit guides" like our guardian angel and other personal spirit guides. After I realized what this crystal was all about, I began meditating with it. Every time I meditate and a new spiritual being comes to me during meditation, I always ask who is this or what is his/her name. The devic crystal is a channel for the devas, and they quickly told me they are there to provide information and guidance; however, they are not my personal spiritual guides. In that case, they would never tell me their names. Plus, different ones come through each time I use it.

If I ask questions that I am not allowed to know the answer to at that time, they will tell me so. That is true with all of the spirit guides I have met during meditation. If I am meant to have the answer at the time, they will provide as much information as needed. If I am not meant to have the answer at that time, they will flat out tell me that this is not the time for me to have the answer. So I got used to just using this crystal as what it was meant to be used for, a channel for information and guidance with no personal attachments or connections. Some of the deva spirits can be very straightforward and factual, some more friendly, while others even have a bit of a sense of humor, but none of them have ever told me their names as my own personal spirit guides have.

If you want to try working with a devic temple crystal, hold the crystal in your hand or place it by your side and then go into your meditative state by relaxing and clearing your mind. Once you clear your mind and you feel the energy from the crystal, just be open to receiving information; then you can begin to ask the devas questions. You can ask questions regarding information that can help you with your journey. You can also ask about why you are experiencing certain situations. You really are unlimited with what you can ask, and remember, they will tell you if you are not allowed to have information on that subject at that time. You may receive answers as a voice, vision, or a knowing. It would be a good idea to journal these sessions as well.

Euphoralite

In 2019, I was introduced to another very high vibration crystal called euphoralite by a good friend of mine. I had never heard of it before and there is not much information available on it except websites where others have posted their experiences with it. I was intrigued and decided I needed to find out about this crystal for myself, so I contacted the owner of the mine in South Dakota and got first hand information and purchased several pieces to work with. There are five variations (purple, yellow, lilac, snowball, and red dragon) of euphoralite which contain up to forty different minerals. The more prominent minerals found in the five variations are blue tourmaline, lithium, lepidolite, quartz, feldspar and mica. The combinations of these minerals brings this crystal to a very high vibration.

My first time meditating session with this crystal was something I have never experienced before. I felt what I can only describe as an electrical charge all around my body. I was vibrating from head to toe, and my body was pulsing to the beating of my heart. I saw myself surrounded in white universal light, and I could feel the cleansing and clearing of my being. Afterwards I felt dizzy so I had to ground myself with black tourmaline. I have incorporated euphoralite into my deep meditations since and by doing so I have been given profound guidance, and I have been able to reach deeper levels within my being than I ever have before. This crystal is definitely here to assist us with our spiritual evolution.

Euphoralite can provide multi level healing and spiritual guidance but start off slowly and work your way into getting used to its energy. If you would like to work with euphoralite, select the variety that you are drawn to most. I suggest you hold one in each hand during meditation, and when you feel comfortable with its energy, begin to add one to your third eye as well. If you have all five varieties, hold one in each hand, place one on your third eye, and use your intuition as to where to place the other two. Go into meditation with the question of "what do I need to know at this time?" or ask for specific guidance. You may experience intense energy surrounding you or throughout your body. You may see colors or visions, or hear guidance. Be open to what is given to you during these sessions. Make sure to ground yourself if you feel the need after each session using euphoralite. This crystal can take you places you quite possibly never dreamed of!

If you are interested in taking your spiritual journey deeper, try a higher-vibration crystal. The ones mentioned above are just a few of many that can assist you with that goal. Some help with time travel, astral projection, teleportation, channeling, past-life connection, and so much more. I have experienced all of those areas listed through meditation, and you can too. Just take your meditative journey one step at a time and try to have realistic goals. These things rarely happen overnight so to speak. Give it time to develop into a deeper spiritual journey and trust the process as you practice meditation. It really depends on what you want to experience or learn.

Remember, if you use a higher-vibration crystal or master crystal, you may want to consider placing a protective Universal light around you to protect you during your meditative session so only light and love come through. After your sessions with master crystals, you may feel a little dizzy or lightheaded, so you will need to ground yourself if that is the case. Take a look at the following chapter on grounding to be prepared if you need to ground yourself.

Chapter 11

Grounding

Sometimes after a deep meditation or if you are not used to crystal energy, you may feel a little dizzy or lightheaded. After my first time using a high-vibration crystal, I felt a bit dizzy because I was not used to the higher energy. This can happen but not necessarily to everyone. If you do feel dizzy or lightheaded after meditation, you should ground yourself afterward.

What is Grounding

What is grounding? Grounding is to become stable and rebalanced again. Although this is more geared toward meditation, you can use these suggestions for any time you may feel dizzy, lightheaded, out of balance, or just having an "off" or out-of-sorts type of day. I am personally affected by buildings that have a lot of fluorescent lighting or electronics, which cause me to be dizzy. So I will carry a grounding crystal with me when I enter such places to keep me balanced and stable.

Crystals to Use for Grounding

Here is a list of some crystals that can help with grounding. You will not need all of them; just choose the ones that resonate with you and see which ones work best for you. Of course, this is not a comprehensive list either, so if you are looking for more, please refer to your crystal references. I have found that these crystals work very effectively and quickly. (The crystals listed below are referenced from *The Crystal Bible*.)

- Black tourmaline
- Smoky quartz
- Hematite
- Fairy stone
- Petrified wood
- Obsidian
- Onyx
- Lodestone
- Shungite
- Pyrite

How to Ground Yourself

There are a few different techniques to help you get grounded.

First, the best and most effective way to get grounded is to place your bare feet upon the ground and connect with the earth. Stand in the dirt, grass, sand, or whatever natural terrain you are able to. It works quickly, and if you are able to place one of these crystals between your feet, it speeds up the process. If you are unable to be outside, then place your bare feet upon the ground indoors with one of your chosen grounding crystals between your feet. Close your eyes and visualize yourself being anchored deep within the earth's core. See a cord attaching you to the core of the earth and feel the steadiness it provides. Do this for about five to ten minutes and then gauge how you feel. If you need a bit of extra time, it is better to listen to your body and give it the extra time.

Another method is to place a grounding crystal between your feet as you lie down for five to ten minutes and just visualize yourself being anchored and stable upon the earth.

You can also hold a grounding crystal in your hand for a quick five- to ten-minute quick hold. Follow the quick-hold meditative process in chapter 7.

If you have an intense feeling of dizziness or lightheadedness, you can lie down and surround your body with a few grounding stones for about ten minutes.

After a few times, you will get to know what grounding crystals are your favorite to work with, and you will get to know what technique works best for you too. The more you work with crystals and meditate with them, the more you will get used to their energies. Everyone is different and unique, so everyone will respond differently. Some people may need grounding more often, some occasionally, and even some not at all.

Chapter 12

Lucid Meditation

Lucid meditation is quite similar to lucid dreaming and self-hypnosis. Lucid dreaming is defined as "a dream during which the dreamer is aware of dreaming. During lucid dreaming, the dreamer may be able to exert some degree of control over the dream characters, narrative, and environment" (Wikipedia). Lucid meditation is very similar; you are aware of being in meditation while in meditation, with the purpose to try to access a specific time or place and exert control of the outcome of the situation involved.

Lucid meditation is quite similar to the hypnotic state as well. During hypnosis, a hypnotherapist will start you on a guided journey, and then your subconscious will go from there. He or she will take you into a deep relaxation and then begin you on a guided journey very similar to guided meditations. Then depending on the prompts he or she has, he or she will ask you to notice specifics on that journey, and then you can continue on that journey on your own. According to

Wikipedia, hypnosis is "an artificially induced trance state resembling sleep, characterized by heightened susceptibility to suggestion." By going into meditation with the intention of accessing the state of lucid meditation and by using a crystal attuned for the journey, similar outcomes of accessing other times and space can be achieved.

Have you ever seen the movie *Somewhere in Time* with Christopher Reeve? His character went into self-hypnosis to time travel to a specific time and place to meet a woman he was obsessed with. Lucid meditation is very similar in a way of obtaining that deep state on the subconscious level to travel to different times and places. Lucid meditation can take some practice to achieve what you want, but the journey itself can be an amazing experience. It is almost like a movie that you create during meditation.

You can do this for past-life recall to heal current-life karma or even travel back to current-life events to heal issues associated with those events. You can also use lucid meditation to time travel, travel to different places around the world or other planets, or even travel to other realms. It is really unlimited in what you can experience.

Past Life Focus

If you focus your intent to access past lives during meditation, you can return to those past lives to recreate the outcomes or sever any vows or attachments that may have been causing you blocks during this lifetime or even future lives. If you have been working on past-life recall, you will have a starting point of what past life you would like to revisit during your lucid meditation session. So for example, say you learned of a past life where you were in extreme poverty your whole life during that lifetime. Maybe you were a slave and in very poor conditions or maybe you were an orphan and had no home or family. Whatever the case may be, you can return to that specific past life and recreate the ending to be very positive. In your meditative state, recreate the circumstances in that specific past life in some way so that you find yourself happy, healthy, and prosperous. You can also view any contracts or vows you may have made from that past life and place a completion or ending upon them so they will no longer continue. While you are there, you can also clear any karma that may have carried over to your current life so that you can be free of any attachments or cords from that past life.

Current Life Focus

You can also practice lucid meditation to heal current-life issues from challenging times you may have experienced. Maybe you are suffering from something, and you really do not understand or remember the root cause of it. I experienced a troubling time in my adult years trying to overcome self-doubt. At the time, I really had thought I had healed so much in my life, and I was actually surprised that self-doubt came to be an issue, but it was something that I could not seem to overcome. So I went into meditation with the intent to see what the cause was, and I found out that it was during a time when I was young and I was suffering from extreme lack of confidence. It brought me back to when I was in the third grade and I was very unhappy with my situation at home. I saw in the meditation exactly how it was back then, how I looked and dressed, and how deep sadness was reflected on my face. Going back to that time and space, I realized that I still needed to focus on healing the events that led to that deep sadness that the younger me was suffering from. So while I was in that meditative state, I used the lucid meditation technique to recreate that time of my life to have a more positive outcome. During the meditation, I forgave those who caused me heartache and pain and recreated the outcome for me to be more outgoing, self-confident, and happy. Once I finished the meditation, I actually felt lighter and free of the bonds of self-doubt. I felt I had released the block that was holding me back in the present time.

Lucid Meditation Process

To do this type of meditation, select a high-vibration or master crystal that works well with past-life recall or time travel and hold it in your hand or set it next to you during meditation. Follow the relaxation techniques and go into your meditation with the intention of accessing a specific past life (or current life experience if that is your intent) you want to work on recreating. Focus on going back into that time and space and recreate the outcome to be more positive. These types of meditations may require grounding afterward, so be prepared to ground yourself if it is needed. I say this often and I will say it again: Everyone is different, and everyone will respond differently. Of course, these types of meditations can bring up certain emotions that need to be released, and that can be part of the overall process. Plus, this is not a substitute for medical or psychological care; however, if you are experienced in meditation and it is something you wish to explore, it is mentioned here as an option. There may be some challenging times in your life that you may not be ready to revisit, so be mindful of that as well.

You can also use lucid meditation to explore new worlds, past creations, and future worlds and lives. It can take you wherever you would like to go if you are open to it. Some crystals to help you with this process would be a time link, Cathedral Lightbrary, elestial, Lemurian, euphoralite, rainbow quartz, or most any other high-vibration crystal associated with past-life recall or deep meditation. I would recommend to really get a good feel for daily meditation and the feel for higher-vibration crystals before you attempt lucid meditation just because it can be a bit more challenging to achieve. Some may be able to achieve this more easily than others do, especially if you already have experienced deep meditation, lucid dreaming, or hypnosis. In those cases, it would be most likely that you can tap into that deeper state of meditation much quicker and easier because you have a sense of what it can be like. I do not want to dissuade you from trying it; I am just being realistic.

Chapter 13

Final Thoughts

Meditation with crystals can open up a whole new world to you. You can work on self-healing for most any issues you dealing with. You can also work with crystals to bring you to a deep state of peace and calmness each day. That in itself has profound healing effects. You can also use it for daily guidance and wisdom from your higher power (God, Creator, or Universe). Or even a combination of self-healing and guidance. Use the information given as a guide to start, and then take it from there.

We are all different and respond differently, so try a few of the mentioned techniques and suggestions and then use what works best for you. There is no limit to what you can gain from meditation, and I have found that using crystals with meditation has amplified the effects of meditation tremendously. Incorporating crystals into meditation can make it easier to clear your mind and take you to a deeper state of meditation. Plus, you receive the healing benefits from the crystals at the same time.

Experiment with different crystals to see which ones work best for you. You will get a good feel for the crystal energy that resonates with you the most, and you will probably find the "go-to" crystal that you tend to use quite often.

Remember, there are no rules for meditation. All you have to do is devote the time, and in a short amount of time with practice, you should start to see positive changes in your life. The more time you put into it, the more you will get out of it. You may find that this is something that you begin to do every day. I wish you all the best in your new meditative journey.

Bibliography

Dictionary.com. 2017 www.dictionary.com

Hall, Judy. *The Crystal Bible*: A Definitive Guide to Crystals Vol. 1. Cincinnati:Walking Stick Press, 2003.

Healingcrystalsforyou.com. s.v. "High Vibration Crystals" 2006-2017 https://www.healing-crystals-for-you.com/crystal-energy.html

Merriam-Webster.com. s.v. "Telepathy" 2017 www.merriam-webster.com/dictionary/

Proctor, Bob.*The Secret.* Directed by Drew Heriot. Australia: Prime Time Productions, 2006.

Raphaell, Katrina. *The Crystalline Transmission: A Synthesis of Light,* Vol. 3. SantaFe:Aurora Press, 1990.

Reeve, Christopher. *Somewhere in Time.* Directed by Jeannot Szware. United States: Universal Pictures, 1980.

Shutterstock.com 2017 Licenced Images https://www.shutterstock.com

Simmons, Robert, and Naisha Ahsian. *The Book of Stones: Who They Are and What They Teach*, Revised and Expanded Edition. Berkley:North Atlantic Books, 2015.

Wikipedia. s.v. "Lucid Dreams." Last modified October 12, 2017. https://en.wikipedia.org/wiki/Lucid_dream.

Acknowledgments

I have so much gratitude in my heart for being able to create this book, and I wish to give heartfelt thanks to all those who have helped me along my journey. This includes but is not limited to the following people:

Elisa Lee, thank you for creating such a beautiful image to include on this publication. I deeply appreciate your friendship and support, thank you for always being there. I look forward to future projects with you!

I want to thank my mentors Hibiscus Moon and Sal Jade for their support over the years. I am so grateful I followed my guidance and took your courses!

I want to thank all my friends and family who listened to me when I needed someone to talk to, who picked me up when I was doubtful, and who have always been there regardless of my point of view. Thank you for your support.

I also want to thank my Facebook fans, friends, and followers. You have made my life richer in so many ways. Thank you for your kindness, friendship, and support. I have learned so much from you, and I am so grateful we have created a community among ourselves.

I want to extend thanks to all of my clients and students over the years. Thank you for allowing me to be part of your healing journey. I am truly humbled to be working with you.

Thank you, dear spirit guides and God, most of all for being with me every step of the way during my journey. They kept telling me to trust the process and I am so glad I did. I am grateful that I found such a deep connection with the Divine, one that continues to grow each day.

Last but not least, I want to thank all of you who purchased this book. One of my passions has become to help everyone learn to meditate, so I hope that I was able to help you achieve that in some way.

Glossary

Astral projection: the act of separating the astral body (spirit or consciousness) from the physical body and its journey into the universe

Chakra: energy wheel in Sanskrit, it is a spinning vortex of energy; they are centers in the human energy field which distributes the energy that supports the functioning of the body, mind and emotions (*The Crystal Bible, pg 379*)

Channeling: the practice of professedly entering a meditative or trancelike state in order to convey messages from a spiritual guide (dicionary.com)

Deva: a higher being or god

Grounding: to become stable and steady

Guided meditation: a meditation session conducted with verbal instruction from a teacher

High-vibration crystals: crystals that have higher frequencies and stronger energy fields (*healingcrystalsfor you.com*)

Karma: bringing upon oneself inevitable results, good or bad, in this lifetime or reincarnation

Layout (crystal): an arrangement of specific crystals around the body for a specific outcome

Lucid dreaming: being aware of dreaming while you are dreaming

Lucid meditation: meditative state to try to access a specific time or place and exert control of the outcome of the situation involved, and being aware of being in meditation while in meditation

Mantra: a sound, syllable, word, phrase, or sentence used as a chant during prayer or meditation

Master crystals: crystals that align with the Divine, which allows access to higher realms and dimensions (*The Crystalline Transmission p.125*)

Meditation: to engage in mental exercise (such as concentration on one's breathing or repetition of mantra) for reaching a heightened level of spiritual awareness

Past-life recall: a technique to recover what practitioners believe are memories of past lives or incarnations

Spirit guides: a spirit on the spiritual plane who guides a spirit having a human experience on the physical plane

Telepathy: transmission of information from one person to another without using any of our known sensory channels or physical interaction (*merriam-webster.com*)

Teleporting: transfer of matter or energy from one point to another without traversing the physical space between them

Universal white light: the space within the Universe that houses positive energies

Visualization: the formation of a mental image of something

More Fun Crystal Stuff

Would you like to learn more about crystals and ways to use them in practical easy ways?

Enroll in my course

"Exploring Basic Ways to Use Crystals For Your Well-being"

In this course we explore how crystal energy works, how to select and care for crystals, and how to meditate with them. Plus, we will also explore the seven major Chakra's and what crystals are associated with balancing those, and I discuss my top ten favorite crystals and why I think everyone should have them in their tool kit. I have even provided a recorded guided meditation that you can use anytime you like!

To enroll go to Udemy.com and enter the course title or my name.

Would you like to join a positive spiritual community that focuses on crystals, angels, and spiritual growth? Join me on my

Facebook page facebook.com/dhardyacm1

If you would like to join a group of like minded people on their spiritual path my Facebook group **Crystalline Sage** is the place for you. This is a safe place where you can discuss your spiritual journey with others without judgement.

If you are interested in distance healing sessions, visit my website at
www.hardycrystalblessing.com
to book your session.

Sessions may include re-alignment of your energetic frequencies and/or removal of any emotional and energetic blocks. This type of energy healing can promote good health in our physical, emotional, mental and spiritual bodies. I use Crystal, Reiki and Angel energy during healing sessions.

Made in the USA
Las Vegas, NV
27 March 2021